Totally WACKY FACTS ABOUT the MIND

CARI MEISTER

CAPSTONE PRESS
a capstone imprint

THE BRAIN IS LIKE MISSION CONTROL FOR THE ENTIRE BODY.

YOU CAN'T DANCE WITHOUT YOUR BRAIN.

No one understands exactly how the mind works.

YOU CAN'T EVEN BREATHE WITHOUT YOUR BRAIN!

A BABY'S SKULL IS PARTLY OPEN TO MAKE ROOM FOR ITS BRAIN (AND MIND) TO GROW.

A baby's brain doubles in size in the first year.

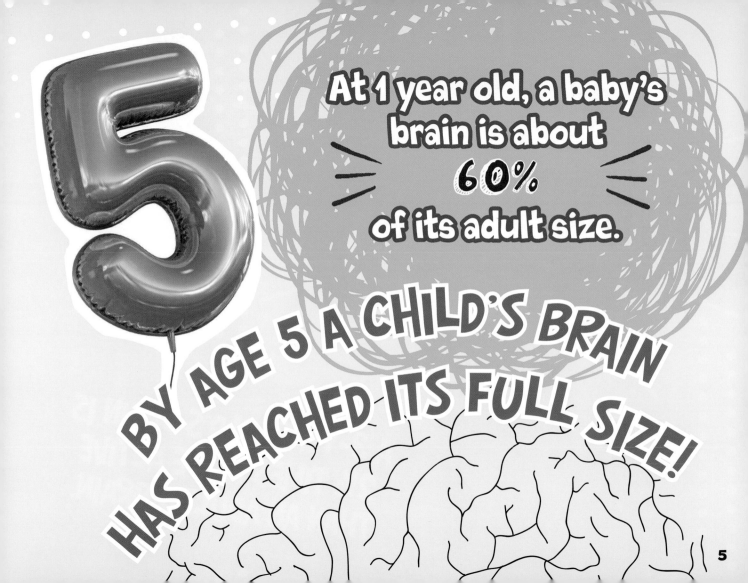

5

At 1 year old, a baby's brain is about **60%** of its adult size.

BY AGE 5 A CHILD'S BRAIN HAS REACHED ITS FULL SIZE!

LEARNING NEW THINGS HELPS YOUR BRAIN GROW.

A 3-YEAR-OLD'S BRAIN IS 2½ TIMES MORE ACTIVE THAN AN ADULT'S BRAIN.

ONE STUDY SAYS THE BRAINS OF MEN AND WOMEN ARE WIRED DIFFERENTLY.

Women and men use different brain parts to do the same activities.

THE AVERAGE BRAIN WEIGHS ABOUT 3 POUNDS (1.36 KILOGRAMS) AND IS THE SIZE OF A CANTALOUPE.

ON AVERAGE, MEN HAVE BIGGER BRAINS THAN WOMEN.

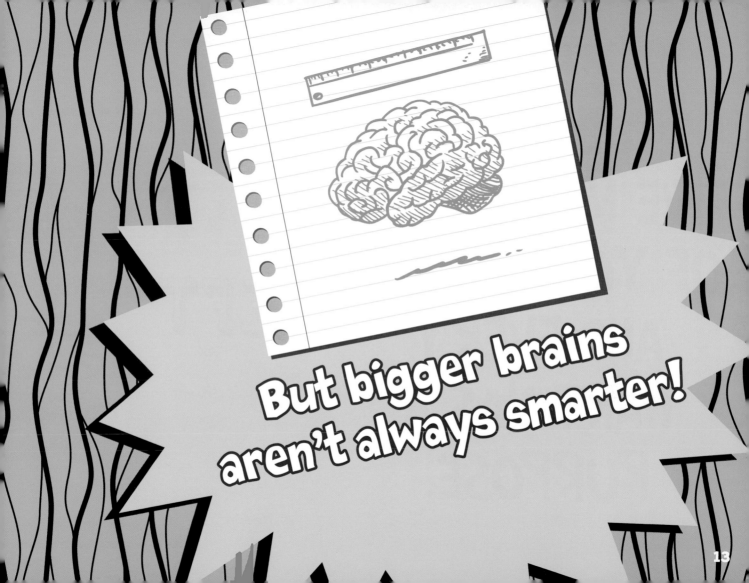

But bigger brains aren't always smarter!

THERE ARE FIVE MAIN PARTS OF YOUR BRAIN, AND EVERY PART HAS A PURPOSE.

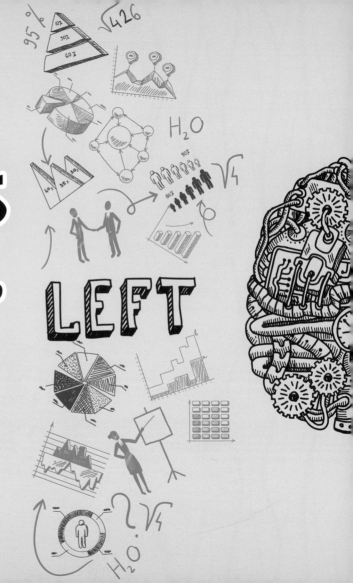

Right

EACH SIDE
OF YOUR BRAIN
CONTROLS THE
OPPOSITE
SIDE OF
YOUR BODY.

The BRAIN itself does not feel PAIN.

There's a thermometer in your head—the **hypothalamus!**

THE PEARL-SIZED PART CONTROLS YOUR TEMPERATURE.

A BRAIN PART CALLED THE AMYGDALA HELPS YOU READ OTHER PEOPLE'S EMOTIONS.

It's also the part that tells you to SCREAM when you're scared!

21

Like monarch butterflies, humans may have an internal compass.

CAN WE TRAVEL ACROSS THE GLOBE WITHOUT HELP FROM A MAP?

YOUR BRAIN FEELS KIND OF LIKE SLIMY GELATIN.

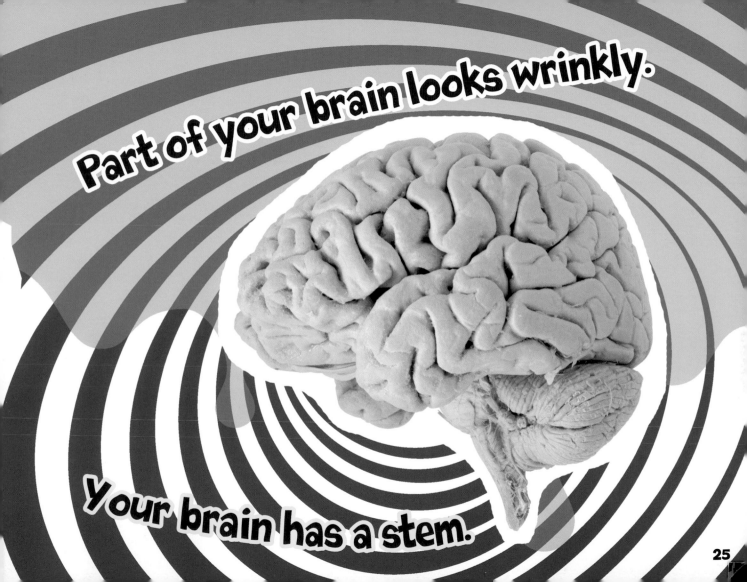

Part of your brain looks wrinkly.

Your brain has a stem.

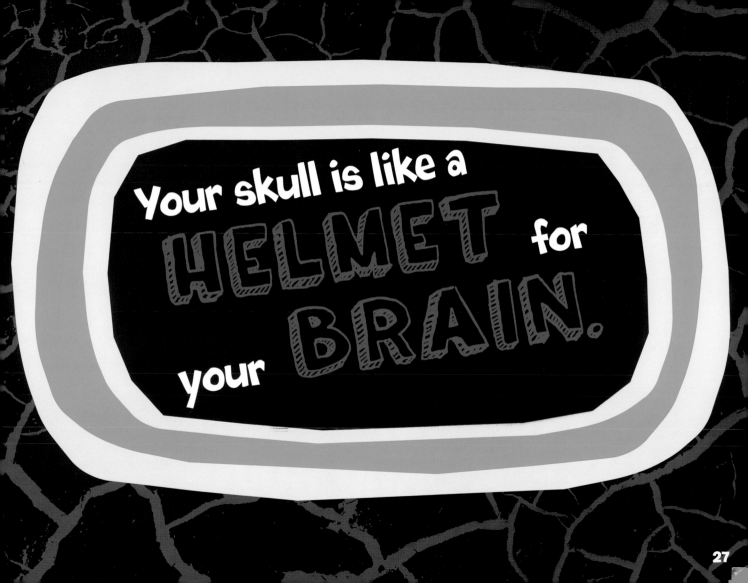

Your skull is like a HELMET for your BRAIN.

There are about 86 billion neurons in your brain.

NEURONS TRANSMIT ALL KINDS OF INFORMATION ALL OVER YOUR BODY.

It would take you more than three years to count all your neurons!

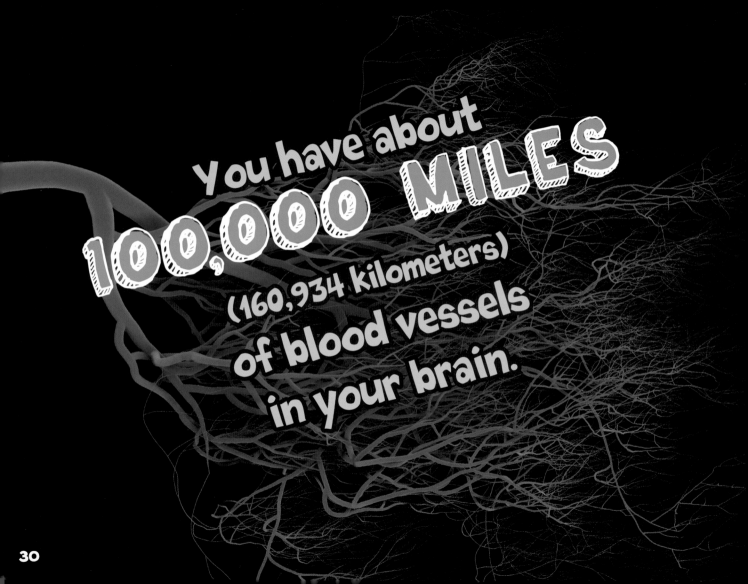

You have about
100,000 MILES
(160,934 kilometers)
of blood vessels
in your brain.

EVERY MINUTE
ABOUT THREE
SODA CANS
WORTH OF BLOOD
FLOW TO
THE BRAIN.

YOUR BRAIN MAKES ENOUGH ENERGY TO POWER A LIGHTBULB.

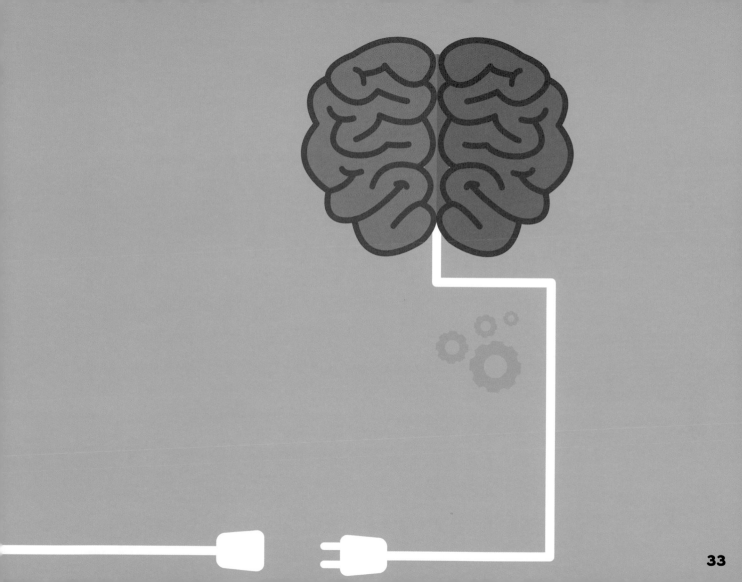

The outside of your brain is pink.

Parts of the brain are white.

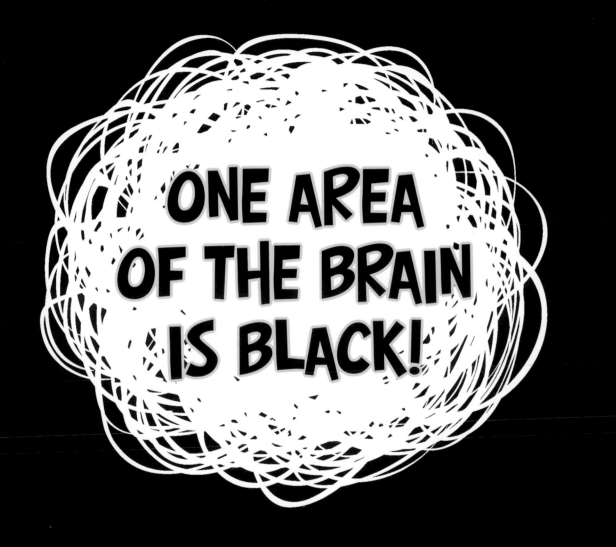

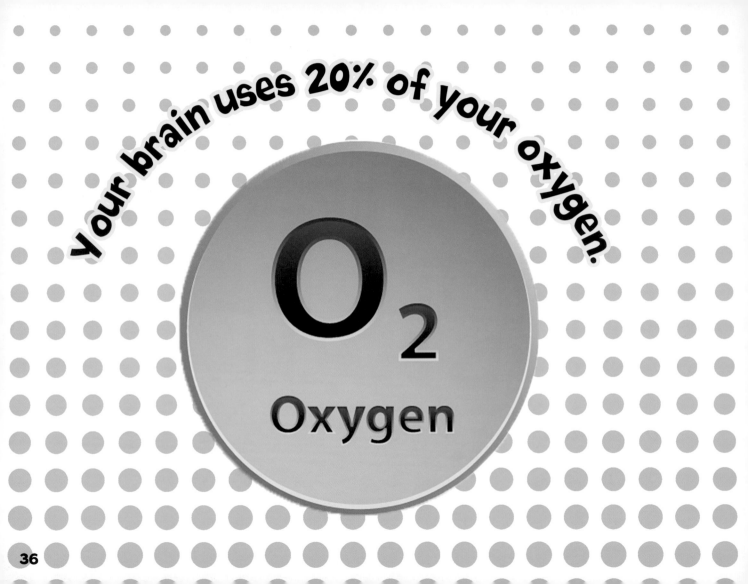

Your brain uses 20% of your oxygen.

O_2

Oxygen

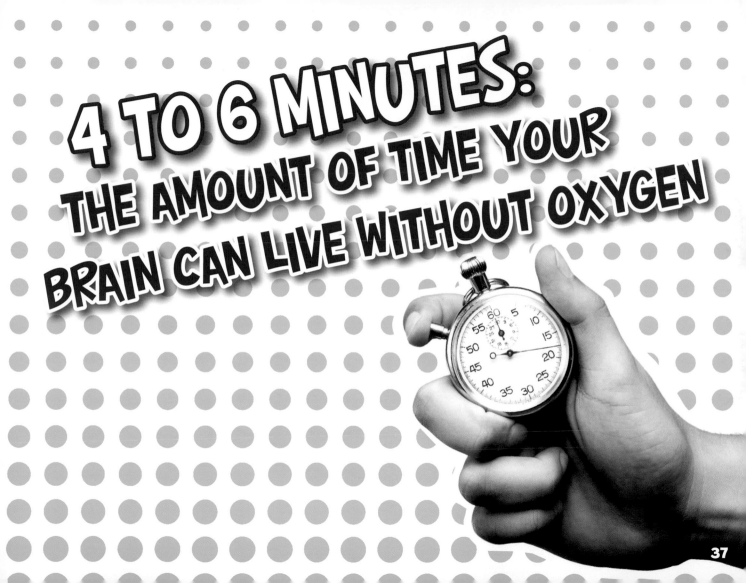

4 TO 6 MINUTES: THE AMOUNT OF TIME YOUR BRAIN CAN LIVE WITHOUT OXYGEN

THE UNITED STATES HAS PERFORMED MORE LOBOTOMIES THAN ANY OTHER COUNTRY.

60% OF YOUR BRAIN IS FAT.

Your brain will eat itself if your diet is missing important nutrients.

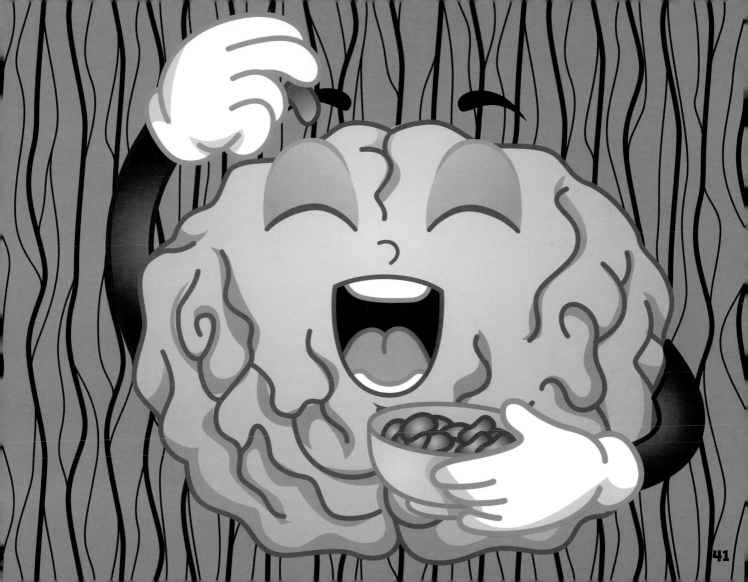

IT'S A MYTH THAT WE USE ONLY 10% OF OUR BRAIN.

Throughout a single day, we actually use all parts of the brain.

BRAINS HAVE NOT BEEN TRANSPLANTED YET, BUT SOME DAY THEY COULD BE!

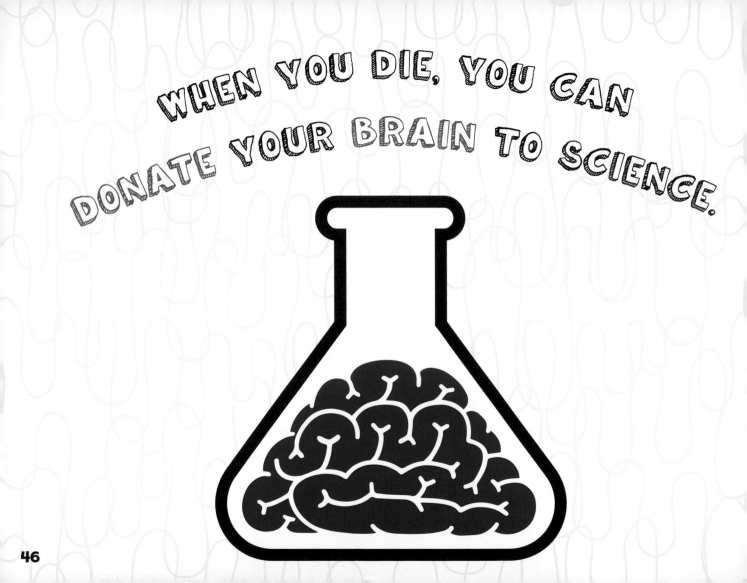

HARVARD UNIVERSITY KEEPS A BRAIN BANK OF ABOUT 3,000 BRAINS.

Your brain can process information very quickly—about 268 miles (431 km) per hour.

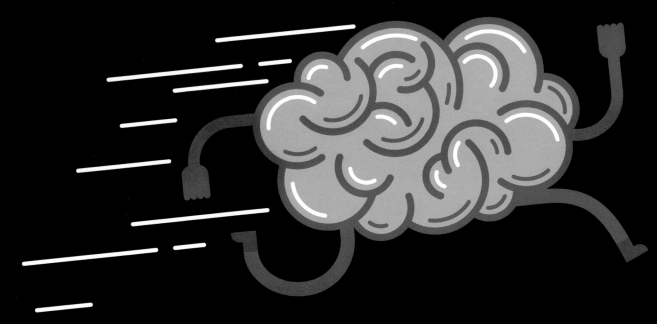

Your body can sense **11 MILLION** bits of information per second.

You can process only about **40** of them.

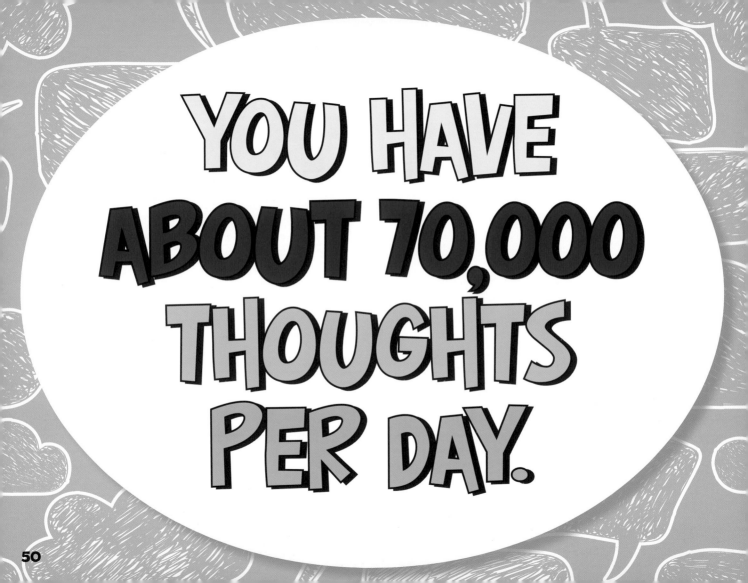

DAYDREAMING IS GOOD FOR YOUR MIND.

The average person daydreams about 47% of the day.

Daydreaming helps your brain make new connections.

A PHYSICAL PATH IS MADE IN YOUR BRAIN WHENEVER YOU HAVE A THOUGHT.

The more times you have had a thought, the easier it is to have again.

THINK GOOD THOUGHTS!
IT WILL MAKE YOU
A HAPPIER PERSON.

Only about **10%** of the population is left-handed.

MICHELANGELO AND DA VINCI WERE LEFT-HANDED.

A STUDY SAYS THAT LEFT-HANDERS DO BETTER ON HIGH-STAKES TESTS.

It also said that lefties get scared more easily than righties.

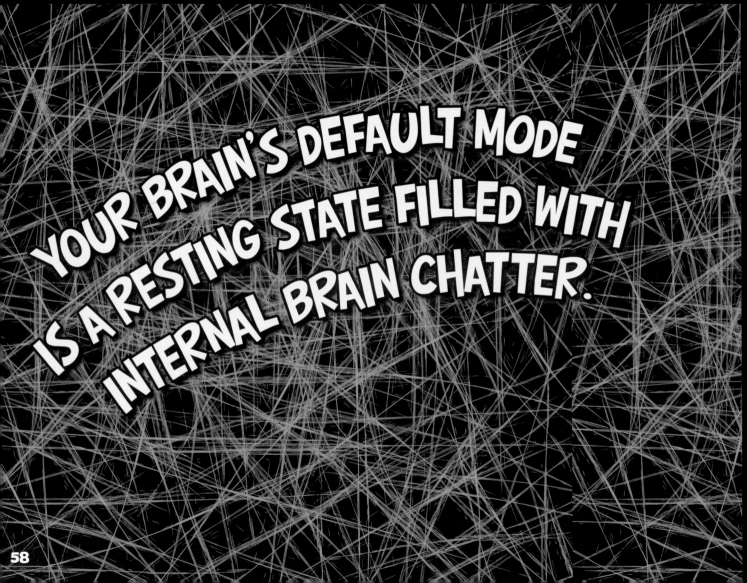

YOUR BRAIN'S DEFAULT MODE IS A RESTING STATE FILLED WITH INTERNAL BRAIN CHATTER.

In this resting state, your brain uses a lot of energy!

YOUR MEMORY OF SOMETHING IS OFTEN WRONG.

Things we see all the time can be easily forgotten because we see them so often.

Your brain changes your memories when you talk about them.

SOME PEOPLE BELIEVE THEIR MINDS CAN PREDICT THE FUTURE. THEY'RE CALLED CLAIRVOYANTS.

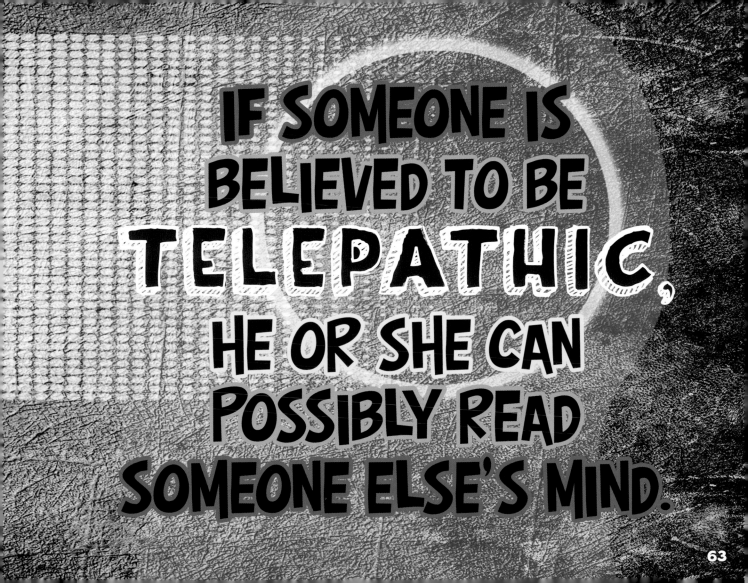

IF SOMEONE IS BELIEVED TO BE **TELEPATHIC,** HE OR SHE CAN POSSIBLY READ SOMEONE ELSE'S MIND.

ESP stands for "extra sensory perception."

PEOPLE WHO THINK THEY HAVE ESP BELIEVE THEY CAN SENSE THINGS WITH THEIR MINDS.

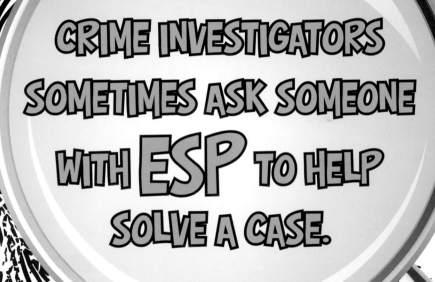

CRIME INVESTIGATORS SOMETIMES ASK SOMEONE WITH ESP TO HELP SOLVE A CASE.

Déjà vu is kind of like a brain hiccup. It happens when there is a brain malfunction.

SOME PEOPLE BELIEVE DÉJÀ VU HAPPENS WHEN TWO UNIVERSES COLLIDE.

DÉJÀ VU MEANS "ALREADY SEEN" IN FRENCH.

Jigsaw puzzles

exercise parts of the brain.

THERE IS NO SUCH THING AS A TRULY PHOTOGRAPHIC MEMORY.

Some people can memorize the order of a deck cards in under one minute.

COLORS CAN INSPIRE OUR BRAINS TO THINK IN A CERTAIN WAY.

The color blue sparks **CREATIVITY.**

The color green makes people feel relaxed.

A TEENAGER NEEDS 9¼ HOURS OF SLEEP FOR HIS BRAIN TO FUNCTION PROPERLY.

If you get good sleep, you will get better grades.

MOST TEENAGERS IN THE UNITED STATES DON'T GET ENOUGH SLEEP.

Some people say you can't DREAM and SNORE at the same time.

NUMBER OF DREAMS IN A LIFETIME:

100,000

EVERYONE DREAMS. YOU JUST FORGET MOST OF YOUR DREAMS.

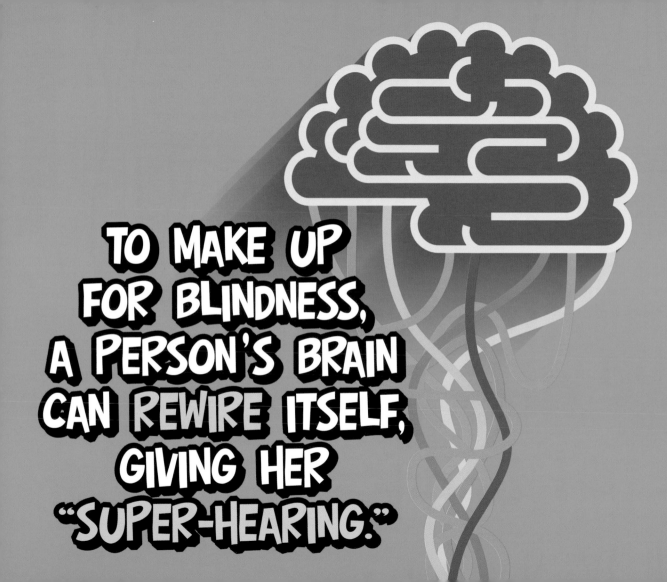

TO MAKE UP FOR BLINDNESS, A PERSON'S BRAIN CAN REWIRE ITSELF, GIVING HER "SUPER-HEARING."

REAL LAUGHTER HAPPENS UNCONSCIOUSLY.

Laughter activates five different parts of the brain.

IN CREATIVE THINKING,
THERE IS NEVER ONE ANSWER.

To be creative,
you must practice
being creative.

A recent study found there is a network over a large area of the brain that is used during creative thinking.

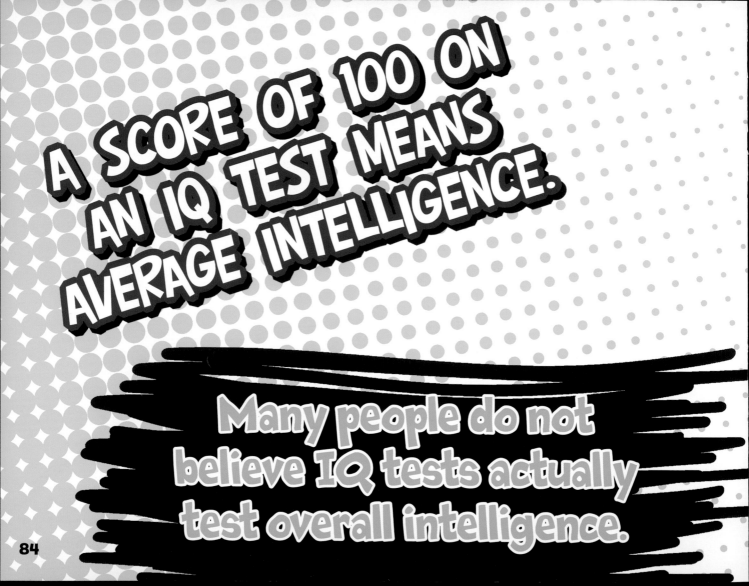

A SCORE OF 100 ON AN IQ TEST MEANS AVERAGE INTELLIGENCE.

Many people do not believe IQ tests actually test overall intelligence.

HIGHEST ADULT IQ ON RECORD: 198

Music can transport your mind back in time.

Musical training helps some children improve their reading.

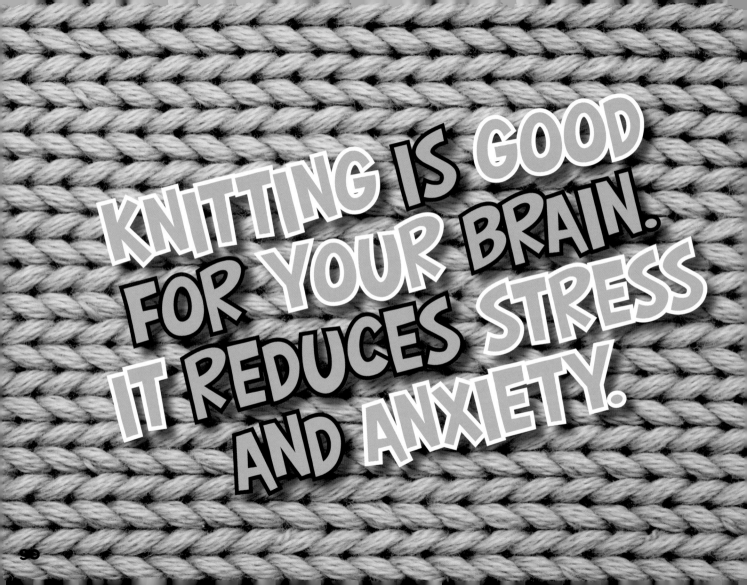

LIKE PUZZLES, BRAIN GAMES HELP TO IMPROVE YOUR ABILITY TO REASON.

OPTICAL ILLUSIONS TRICK THE BRAIN.

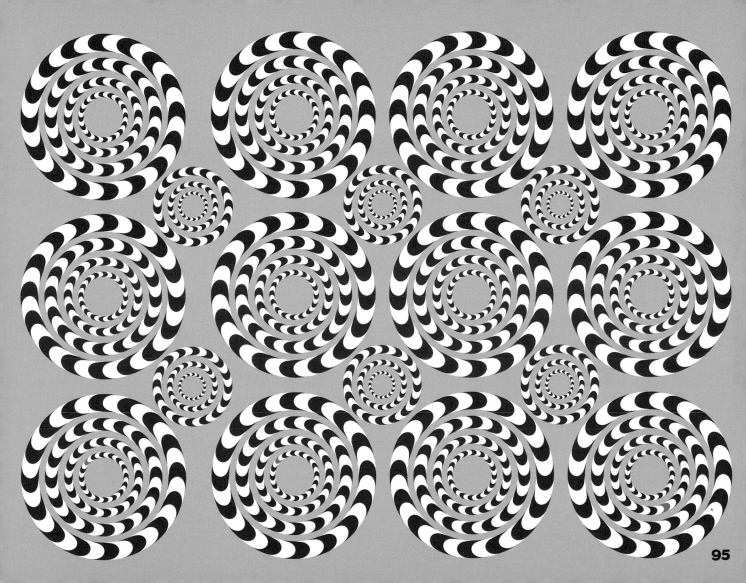

95

Reading to kids makes them smarter.

If you read 20 minutes a day, you will be exposed to 1.8 million words per year!

People who read for fun do better in school.

When you see someone hit his head, the same pain area in your brain lights up.

Smelling chocolate has a RELAXING effect on your mind.

EATING CHOCOLATE SENDS A RUSH OF BLOOD TO AREAS OF YOUR BRAIN.

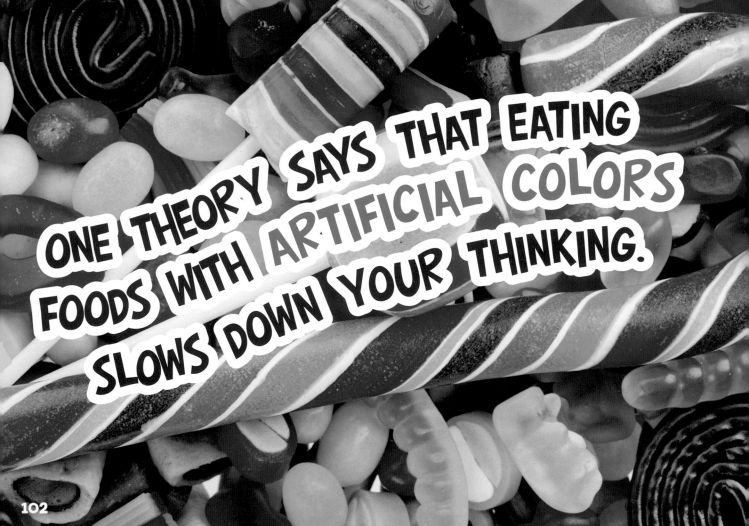

ONE THEORY SAYS THAT EATING FOODS WITH ARTIFICIAL COLORS SLOWS DOWN YOUR THINKING.

Highly processed foods trick your brain into wanting more.

ABOUT 90% OF SICKNESS AND DISEASE IS RELATED TO STRESS IN YOUR MIND.

BEING PHYSICALLY FIT HELPS YOUR BRAIN STAY YOUNG.

You think more clearly after exercising.

Ways to boost your brainpower:

EXERCISE EVERY DAY.

SLEEP WELL.

KEEP LEARNING.

GLOSSARY

amygdala—small groups of cells in your brain that are responsible for your feelings

anxiety—a feeling of worry or fear

hypothalamus—your brain's thermostat

IQ—short for intelligence quotient; a number used to measure someone's intelligence

lobotomy—a surgical operation on the brain

mature—having reached full growth or development

neuron—a nerve cell

optical illusion—something that makes us see things that do not exist or are different than they appear

photographic memory—memory that is capable of retaining information that is as clear as a photograph

process—put through a series of tasks

theory—an idea that explains something that is unknown

transplant—to remove and replace with one that works

trasport—to move from one place to another

READ MORE

Amsel, Sheri. *The Everything Kids Human Body Book: All You Need to Know About Your Body Systems—From Head to Toe!* Avon, Mass.: Adams Media Corp., 2012.

Mason, Paul. *Can You Lick Your Elbow?: And Other Questions About the Human Body.* Chicago: Capstone Raintree, 2014.

Rogers, Simon. *Human Body.* Information Graphics. Somerville, Mass.: Candlewick Press, 2014.

INTERNET SITES

FactHound offers a safe, fun way to find Internet sites related to this book. All of the sites on FactHound have been researched by our staff.

Here's all you do:

Visit *www.facthound.com*

Type in this code: 9711491483619

INDEX

Mind Benders are published by Capstone,
1710 Roe Crest Drive, North Mankato, Minnesota 56003
www.mycapstone.com

Editor: Shelly Lyons
Designer: Lori Bye
Media Researcher: Jo Miller

Library of Congress Cataloging-in-Publication Data
Meister, Cari, author.
Totally wacky facts about the mind / by Cari Meister.
pages cm.—(Mind benders)
Audience: Ages 8-12.
Audience: Grades 4 to 6.
Summary: "Presents more than 100 facts about the human mind
in a unique layout that appeals to struggling and reluctant
readers."— Provided by publisher.
ISBN 978-1-4914-8361-9 (library binding: alk. paper)
ISBN 978-1-4914-8369-5 (paperback: alk. paper)
ISBN 978-1-4914-8371-8 (ebook pdf)
1. Brain—Juvenile literature. 2. Human physiology—Juvenile literature.
3. Thought and thinking—Juvenile literature. I. Title. II.
Series: Mind benders (Capstone Press)

QP376.M494 2016
612.8′2—dc23   2015031028

Photo Credits

Dreamstime: Akulamatiau, Cover, (bottom right), 51; Shutterstock: Aaron Amat, 37, aboikis, Cover, (top right), advent, 13, Africa Studio, 24, Aleksandr Khakimullin, 75, Alexilus, Cover, (bottom left), Andrei Tarchyshnik, 86, Aniwhite, 79, Anna Shkolnaya, 50-51, Bard Sandemose, 57, Blend Images, 11, Cloud7Days, 10-11, Complot, 44, Cory Thoman, 61, Dan Kosmayer, 31, Daxiao Productions, 2, Deborah Kolb, 43, DenisFilm, 89, Dooder, 85, DVARG, 26, Fabio Berti, 38, Flegere, 8-9, Gala, 72, Gelpi JM, 4, glenda, 25, Halfpoint, 7, Halfpoint, 82-83, Hardyguardy, 20-21, (top and bottom), Igor Zh., 42-43, Incomible, 64-65, Ivelin Radkov, 90-91, Iveta Angelova, 67, Johavel, 76, jps, 22, kasahasa, 32-33, Konstantin Inozemtsev, 30, Kostiantyn Fastov, 105, koya979, 5, lanych, 12, Ljupco Smokovski, 104, Ljupco Smokovski, 108, lolloj, 62-63, LongQuattro, 36, Lorelyn Medina, 41, lotan, 95, Lyudmyla Kharlamova, 70-71, Macrovector, 14-15, Madlen, 102, Marco Govel, 101, Maridav, 106, Marie Maerz, 91, matimix, 107, Matthias G. Ziegler, 87, Monkik, 47, Moofer, Cover, (top left), Morphart Creation, 39, musicman, 65, Orhan Cam, 96, PathDoc, 52, Petr Vaclavek, 68-69, pio3, 99, Piotr Marcinski, 21, ra2studio, 55, ratch, 54, Roman Sigaev, 71, RONORMANJR, 3, Sam72, 16, Samuel Borges Photography, 109, Sanjacm, 56, Sergey Furtaev, 81, Sergey Shenderovsky, 59, Shirstok, 48, SoRad, 46, sumire8, 23, totallyPic.com, 92, Valery Sidelnykov, 9, Vector for u, 2-3, VIGE.CO, 18, (bottom), vitstudio, 28, vivat, 18, (top), Vladimir Matvienko, 58-59, wavebreakmedia, 60

Design Elements by Capstone and Shutterstock

Printed in US.
092015 007526GCS